DEACTIVATED WEST 100

DEACTIVATED

WEST 100

Don McKay

GASPEREAU PRESS
Printers & Publishers

2005

In memory of my parents,
John and Margaret McKay

1

Otherwise Than Place

I keep a rubbing stone in my pocket – a piece of glossy basalt from the west coast of Vancouver Island. It's become my palm's companion, always there in moments of stress or boredom, a reassuring weight that's smoother – thanks to the continual wave action which has kept it rubbing against the other rocks on the beach – than skin. Do my fingers, at some level, sense that static energy inside the polish, some residue of the work that went into that gloss, a very local expression of immeasurable force? Its blackness, when I take it out into the light, is darkness with depth, like an eye or a black bear. Sometimes holding it I recall that pebble beach (this is, after all, partly a souvenir) with its huge drift logs heaped against the forest by Pacific winter storms, its edge of staunch Sitka spruce backed by Douglas-fir and Western red cedar, its gradient of rock from boulder (at the end protected by offshore islets) through gravel to pebble to sand. But mostly it's the outcrop rocks I remember – those raw teeth sieving the sea, constantly breaking the surf into fountains of spray or focussing it into surge channels which can concentrate a wave so that it rushes up in a spout. I had my back turned to what I later realized was a surge channel one stormy day while I tried to photograph the mosaic of the beach below, and found myself suddenly shoved, camera first, into the rock face: one casual flick from the Pacific which left me drenched.

To think the connection between my introspective black companion and those outcrop rocks taking the brunt of ocean – this requires a stretch of the imagination, including what is perhaps the supreme stretch test – geologic time. I find it a bit easier when I'm back there on the beach in the middle of the forces that accomplished this transformation, though not much. But I think that stretch, and its failure, are further reasons for keeping this smooth eccentric shape in my pocket, contrasting with the locals – those flat metal disks with their two-dimensional portraits of monarchs, moose, beavers and loons.

Now here's a strange thing I have fallen into: when I do get back there (it's been a few years), I'm going to take this rubbing stone and toss it, as casually as I can manage, back among its fellows. I can make this boast because I've done this three times over the last fifteen years or so, selecting another to be my rubbing stone each time the one my fingers have memorized returns to anonymous rock. On the first occasion I was mostly motivated by practical considerations; having spent an hour engrossed by their individual charms, I realized that, were I to indulge myself, I'd risk trouser-drag. But of course, once performed a few times, something ordinary gets to be habit, gets to be practice, gets to be – down the road – ritual gesture. It's no big deal, but I'm wondering, since I'm trying to think the relation between place and wilderness without going dizzy with abstraction, why it feels right. This set of reflections is a series of runs at an answer.

Let me risk a definition. Suppose we try to define place without using the usual humanistic terms – not home and native land, not little house on the prairie, not even the founding principle of our sense of beauty – but as a function of wilderness. Try this: 'place is wilderness to which history has happened.' Or: 'place is land to which we have occurred.' This would involve asking, for example, not 'what's the beach to me?' but 'what am I to the beach?' Our occurrence to the land – the act which makes place place – could be a major change (homestead, development, resource extraction) or a smaller claim (prospector's stake, survey marker, plastic tape, souvenir stone), but it shifts the relationship; it brings the wild area into the purview of knowledge and makes it – perhaps momentarily, perhaps permanently – a category of mind. "Remember that place we found the huckleberries?"; "Well, I'll tell you where to go if you want to shoot some *real* rapids"; "Now *that's* what I call a nice piece of real estate." Place becomes place by acquiring real or imagined borders and suffering removal from anonymity. Sometimes this seems almost wholly benign. But sometimes it is possible to imagine an inner shudder, akin perhaps to that inward quailing you feel when some authority (the Vice Principal, say, or, for that matter, an author) selects *you* from out of the safe and faceless crowd in which you swam.

What interests me right now – as you can tell from my opening anecdote – are the possibilities for reverse flow in a relationship that has been so thoroughly one-way. The saga of place has involved colonization, agriculture, exploitation, land use, resourcism, and development, sustainable and otherwise. "What we make," Helen Humphreys observes, "doesn't recover from us." I'm not proposing that we can go back, stop farming and living in cities, or undo all the conversions of wilderness to place. But I am suggesting it is good meditative medicine to contemplate otherwise-than-place as a routine thing. Something like a modification of the practice of fishing from trophy hunting to meat acquisition to catch-and-release.

How about this? Porches are parts of houses where place can fray out into its other, where it can be acted upon and invaded – by pigeons, car exhaust, pollen, noise from the teenagers next door. The porch is the ear of the house. Its job is to induce "dwelling," that term in the language of real estate, to work first as a gerund ("dwelling is the art of living along with things"), then as a participle, then as a verb in the active present. It reminds us – if we're not too busy firing up the barbecue – that place is first a matter of perception, then a set of activities, and only latterly walls and a roof. As John Berger points out, home is represented to the homeless not by a house but by "a practice or set of practices" by which a person creates paths in time and space.

Imagining a counter-current to the steady drag of wilderness into place is, from one perspective, to see a spatial category in temporal terms. Place is where stories happen, where undifferentiated time is given human shape, where infinity becomes history. One of our strongest and most primitive claims on land is probably the gravesite, a piece of property devoted, presumably in perpetuity, to the memory of one person, and to that person's story; it becomes, literally, a plot. The marble stone on it might well be seen as an address to infinity (or eternity, its religious cousin) on behalf of historical dwelling. The body in the grave may be rejoining earth, but its name, and story, will live as long as marble. And since we seldom expose ourselves to the bewilderments of geologic time, that looks like forever. Contrary to this may be the gesture of scattering ashes, which implicitly acknowledges process and our participation in it; we join the land in its anonymity. From the vantage point of historical dwelling this goes by the name of oblivion – a name for namelessness, the condition of being unknown or forgotten – a fate we are usually at pains to avoid.

Perhaps fear of oblivion, of having our names perish with our bodies, goes some way to explaining those extremes of our grip on place, which leave the land indelibly marked. In his book *Forests*, Robert Pogue Harrison gives a perceptive account of the opening of the Sumerian Gilgamesh epic. Harrison points out that the hero's motive for wishing to destroy the forest demon is to 'set up his name', which for an ancient Sumerian means having it stamped in brick. Interestingly, when Gilgamesh approaches the sun god, Utu, with his proposal, Utu responds with a question like the one we asked regarding place as a function of wilderness: "… verily thou art, but what art thou to the land?" A durable question, but not one that delays the hero in his willed destruction of the forest and accession to fame. Harrison also notes that Gilgamesh's urge for an enduring name stems from a particular vision of corpses being floated, as was the custom, down the river. This he relates to Utu as the foundation for his desire to clear-cut.

"O Utu, I would enter the 'land', be thou my ally
I would enter the land of the cut-down cedar, be thou my ally."
Utu of heaven answers him:
"… verily thou art, but what art thou to the land?"

"O Utu, a word I would speak to thee, to my word thy ear,
In my city man dies, oppressed is the heart,
Man perishes, heavy is the heart,
I peered over the wall,
Saw the dead bodies ... floating on the river;
As for me, I too will be served thus; verily 'tis so.
Man, the tallest, cannot stretch to heaven,
Man, the widest, cannot cover the earth.
Not (yet) have brick and stamp brought forth the fated end,
I would enter the 'land', I would set up my name."

In Harrison's reading, the cut-down cedars are made to occupy the same space as the human corpses, as they float down the river in the log drive to the city. It isn't greed or the need for building materials that motivates Gilgamesh. Rather, the epic seems to be probing the darkest element in our use of the land – the urge to *lay waste*, to render the material world as matériel, to make of our capacity for destruction an enduring sign and so achieve fame. Or, as Harrison puts it:

> There is too often a deliberate rage and vengefulness at work in the assault on nature and its species, as if one would project onto the natural world the intolerable anxieties of finitude which hold humanity hostage to death. There is a kind of childish furor that needs to create victims in order to exorcise the pathos of victimage within.

Students of the pathology of abuse will probably recognize the shape of this fury as it is expressed in families. And one may also suspect that we are seeing, in this ancient account of heroism, the foundation of the phenomenon known as male rage.

Suppose we take the idea of oblivion and try, as we did with place, to think it from a vantage point outside history. One of its classic statements is Villon's *"Mais où sont les neiges d'antan"*: suppose we carry this question, which is presumed to be rhetorical, in our heads, or enclosed in a slim volume in your backpack (I'm carrying the lunch, after all), while we walk the trail up to the Bow Glacier in Banff National Park. We can park at the viewpoint by Bow Lake (although it might be instructive to walk up the river from, say, Cochrane), take photos of ourselves with Mount Balfour in the background, walk around the lake, through the boulder field and across the recessional moraine, up to Bow Falls (spotting a dipper en route? I hope so) and the foot of the glacier. These *neiges* are truly vintage *d'antan*, dating back to the Wisconsin glaciation, so we have clearly come to the right spot to re-pose Villon's question, which is now obviously not rhetorical, while we munch our trail bars. But the answers, which could begin with the lake and river we've just walked past, proliferate endlessly – not only to everything downstream (Banff, Calgary, the South Saskatchewan, the great plains, Hudson's Bay) but to that hoped-for dipper, those Glacier lilies, that boulder field, and everything touched by the water cycle as it expresses itself in the main ranges of the Rockies and eastward. Oblivion, it seems, is teeming.

For another thought-experiment with oblivion, we could ask about the whereabouts of the shellfish of yesteryear (*"Mais où sont les crustacés d'antan?"*) while we walk to my neighbourhood pub. One of the answers might be the sidewalk under our feet, following the long temporal path which begins with an ammonoid in the Devonian and continues through the death of its organism and the deposition of its shell on the ocean floor, the eventual compacting of those fossils into limestone, the elevation of the limestone beds through shifts in continents or mountain building, the quarrying of the stone, the mixing of the cement, and finally the pouring of the concrete into this here sidewalk, right here on Fairfield Road. Once we get to the pub, we can spend a few minutes sipping our

Okanagan Spring lagers and contemplating the busy-ness of oblivion before – grown somewhat dizzy with it – we turn our attention to gossip and the television, on which the Mariners are leading the Indians with two out in the bottom of the eighth.

Otherwise-than-place, oblivion, geologic time: to contemplate any of these is to countenance our own erasures without rage or despair. I mentioned that I thought such practice good meditative medicine, an antidote to our tendency to make places into permanent memorials of ourselves, whether by monumental construction or unforgettable destruction. But I'm under no illusion that we can dwell in that moment or even rest very long in those icy waters, unless we're candidates for some version of sainthood. The possibility of that anti-humanistic extremity is probably best represented by the persona of the mad trapper who walks away from civilization, shedding all its co-ordinates of identity and place as he goes. I'm thinking in particular of his evocation in Patrick Lane's remarkable long poem *Winter* where the lyric edge speaks directly to the portion of the spirit that craves oblivion, that would walk – or snowshoe – away from name and place and merge with wilderness: a pure antitype to a hero like Gilgamesh, who made the destruction of the forest the making of his name.

> The man without a name who reversed his snowshoes
> and walked forward, head down, shoulders hunched.
> The man who climbed the mountains
> in the heart of winter, crossing the pass,
> heading west into the snow…
>
> Him walking, head down, shoulders hunched, moving
> toward his own quick death, his breath
> breaking sharp and hard,
> entering,
> leaving.

What's needed is, I think, a small dose of this eros of oblivion, the capacity to think backward or forward from place to its mothering wilderness. That might help impede the tendency to manic ownership and keep the relationship flowing both ways. It might help us see our stories dissolving into the infinity of details from which they are made. The inscription fades from the marble, and the marble weeps its minerals into the sea, as surely as the wind will fill those backward snowshoe tracks with snow.

What I miss most about the place I used to live in Lobo Township is the area north of the house which we called the meadow – although bush-in-embryo might have been more appropriate, since I'd planted it with white pine, silver maple, cedars and locusts. Probably I miss it because that was the spot where the permeable membrane between place and its otherwise first became apparent to me, where home acquired a frayed edge. I'd beaten a path around its perimeter, one I still walk in memory, passing through the double row of windbreak spruce and along the drainage ditch, through some brambly blackberry canes to the weeping willows in the corner where the ditch right-angled. Beside it was a large granite boulder I fondly hoped was a glacial erratic, and around it some young spruce which screened it from the road – a natural spot to pause, reflect, and even write, sitting on the not very comfortable bench I built there. I know the kids also used it as some form of hideout at various times, but that belongs to their meadows, not mine.

Our dog, Luke, also liked this spot – shady, secluded, with good access to the drainage ditch with its muskrats and the meadow with its groundhogs. So, after he got hit by the car, we buried him close by. After that happened, I tended to pause here longer. I will always miss him; but let me tell you, that goddam dog would chase anything that moved, and he caught a fair number of them. That was the problem – his discipline was totally compromised by his speed and talent.

Next there was a line of old poplars where I hung a nesting box for kestrels – one of a dozen or so I put up along the concession roads. It seemed quixotic at the time, more of a gesture of homage to a species I loved than a useful move, until one spring, then another, kestrel families moved in. This gave everything more edge, me included. I spent hours when I should have been marking papers watching the fledged birds learning to fly, an accomplishment which posed for the kestrels some of the problems faced by novice skaters. They were endowed, it seemed, with falcon speed but not with the capacity to stop, so they often overflew the perch, braking too late and tumbling over the far side. (Are all beautiful things, caught at awkward moments, so comical?) I met this guy at Hawk Cliff who claimed to have trained one (although you have to wonder who trained whom) to catch pieces of steak he threw up from his barbecue. Sometimes, he said, he'd fake a throw to draw the kestrel's dive, then toss it behind him, the kestrel turning a somersault mid-dive to catch it before it hit the ground. I was hugely envious of this, and briefly considered trying something similar. But what I actually fantasized about was having a kestrel befriend me sufficiently to accompany me to class when I taught "The Windhover" to show those dozy kids how inadequate language was – even hyper-extended Hopkinsese – for those exact and sudden wingbeats.

What am I getting at here? Something like this: each of these stories from the meadow I no longer own (and which has, I'm afraid, moved in the direction of lawn rather than wilderness) gathers place while also recognizing its loss: Luke is becoming earth, the kestrels have long since moved on. Perhaps a form of elegy is implied in all storytelling. I don't know; but I do sense that the process can be as much about letting place go as it is about making it, and ourselves, substantial.

On, then, to the locusts – fast growing, beautifully blooming, very fragile. When an early snow fell one autumn, they caught this unexpected weight in their leaves and bent to the ground. Many snapped. I was busy tending to the damage while Bronwen Wallace was visiting, and of course we were swapping stories. As I recollect, I was standing on a ladder with the chainsaw (bad combination, that) when Bronwen decided to tell the story about the guy whose chainsaw kicked back while he was sawing over his head and embedded itself in his skull. He'd had the presence of mind not to yank it out and unplug the hole, but got himself to Emergency (walking? driving?) with the saw still in his head. True story, so she claimed. Did I finish sawing that locust? Can't recall.

Let me close by risking another pair of definitions: place is the beginning of memory, and memory is the momentary domestication of time. We could continue that walk around the meadow, pausing at the mulberries where the cedar waxwings got drunk, the red maple beloved of orioles, and the grave of the second dog, Sam – and at each the stories would proliferate. But each would come with that temporary, provisional quality built in. Those little walks, whether exercised *in situ* or in memory, exist on the hinge of translation between place and its otherwise, with the flow going both ways, rooting me in place while they simultaneously open – always with that sense of danger, that pre-echo of oblivion – into wilderness.

2

Between Rock and Stone

A GEOPOETIC ALPHABET

In the banquet hall we are toasting our genius at having winnowed thought from wind, we are making speeches, making deals, getting drunk on the prospects of increased information flow and trade. After a while we step outside to observe this wonder close up: a rickety fence made of sticks, a frail hedge against the whatever-it-is beyond. We can poke our noses through and sniff: something like sea tang, something like wolf-willow funk, and something that seems to belong only to the thoughtless wind.

Does meaning mean most when closest to its edge? You come across a glyph carved into the rock and feel the roughsmooth resistance of the sandstone to this sharp, focussed form of erosion, or you sense the excitement and peril of trusting these angled sticks. Back in the banquet hall we are toasting the hypertext, cheering the end of our indenture to the here and now. Out here, now, we can sense the stone reabsorbing the letters into its many deaths and metamorphoses, their edges losing definition, collapsing inward like the month-old hoofprint of a moose. For A is also for astonishment, that widemouthed silence which we occupy, which occupies us as we turn to the immeasurable life of stone.

Most igneous of rocks, basalt is black and mafic –
meaning heavy with iron and magnesium, meaning loyal to the underworld it oozed or spewed
from. Basalt listens to the call of the earth's core,
that closed impacted vowel, and does not concern
itself much with life on the surface, or life, period.
Forced up in rifts and vents, it paves the ocean floor.
Its only thought, as it inches toward return, is down.
When other rocks are washed with rain or sunshine,
they begin to take themselves lightly, and start the
process of assimilating. Even ancient granite will
glisten and be charmed. Basalt just deepens its
sulk. Yet it is thanks to its ancient hexagonal grip
that we have a planet with a nice firm crust and not
some flabby bag of gas. So when you hear the call
of underearth yourself, line your pockets with basalt.
Go down with gravity's dark angel.

To explain how archetypes dwell in mind as potential, unrealized entities, Jung compares their presence to "the axial system of a crystal which preforms the crystalline structure in the mother liquid, although it has no material existence of its own." Since we spend much of our lives in the velvet grip of dreams, we are ready to accept any amount of magic deriving from mind, including the gathering of fierce irresponsible gods out of the very soup of consciousness. But when matter – dumb, brute, supposedly soulless rock – reveals that it too has ontological secrets, that it too is subject to such spiritual seizure, we may well be cast into a condition of empty, symmetrical wonder, as though we had discovered that all the walls in our houses were in fact windows.

Decreation: to make something created pass into the uncreated.
Destruction: to make something created pass into nothingness.
A blameworthy substitute for decreation.

SIMONE WEIL

Some ideas have deep resonance; they reach back in the memory to bring glimmerings, premonitions, intimations into sudden clarity, as though, with their own entry into consciousness, they had simply supplied the candlepower needed to actually light the bulb. Perhaps Weil's idea also had the effect, for me, of giving deeper bite to Keats' negative capability, and carrying it beyond the realm of aesthetics. By resembling destruction, by being its dangerous look-alike, decreation helps me identify one of the paradoxes of creativity – how it cozies up to its opposite, how it always seems to call for some form of *nykia*, some visit to the land of the dead, before it kicks truly into gear. Decreation calls for attention to release its grip on fixed principles, to risk radical not-knowing without succumbing to the seductive currents which go by the name of nihilism.

I found, to my surprise, that I was thinking of decreation when trying to imagine the workings of plate tectonics, especially the subduction of one plate under another. (I live close to a subduction zone on the west side of North America, where its operation, smooth or spastic, directly affects life on the surface.) Generally the heavy oceanic plate is forced under the lighter continental plate, descending to a depth where the heat from the earth's mantle re-melts the rock to magma. This amazing decreative feature of the rock cycle was of course not available to Simone Weil as she wrote about the soul's needful embrace of gravity in the years leading up to World War II, since plate tectonics wasn't generally accepted before the sixties. And surely, I tell myself, the distance between the two realms is too great for any analogy to apply. But such is the deep resonance of these ideas that I still find their reverberations reinforcing one another, insisting against skepticism and the odds that there is an intimate relation between the brief subductions of creativity and the long ruminations of the planet.

Neanderthals, it turns out from comparisons of DNA, are not close to us genetically; they are members of a different species, cousins rather than direct ancestors. We know quite a bit about them because they buried their dead, along with flint tools and meat to use in an afterlife, and so created optimal conditions for their preservation in the fossil record. But of course the last thing the Neanderthals were concerned with, as they interred their lost ones, was being remembered by the aggressive, invasive, technologically advanced species that was going to shove them into extinction. Rather they were making the one gesture that, more than any other, serves to reduce the corrosive power of endless time. The idea of eternity domesticates infinity, nudges it firmly in the direction of place and makes it habitable. "Where Will You Be In Eternity?" the sign asks, implying, as did our Neanderthal cousins, that even the worst of us will be *somewhere*.

Terra Infirma. It isn't just the fear of earthquakes that makes the idea of a fault zone frightening, but the evidence it gives that earth forms and re-forms itself, that its basic *m.o.* is slow catastrophe, not calm. One response to a map of the planet during the Permian, with the enormous landmass of Pangaea sprawled across it, is humour. This, it seems, is pretty low-grade sci-fi. Another, following by a nanosecond, is horror. What violence has occurred to those dear features, the Mediterranean like the mouth's warm cave behind the pursed lips of Gibraltar, the plump praying mantis of Newfoundland, the Aleutians like a trailing cedar bough? Geologically, a fault is any surface along which rocks have moved and broken; imaginatively, it is any fissure through which infinity leaks into history.

When Harry H. Hess published his decisive contributions to the new and controversial theory of plate tectonics in 1962, he had to ask his readers – other geologists – to concede many suppositions in order to entertain the idea that seafloor spreading, driven by magma rising continuously from the mantle, accounts for both the movement of plates and the surprising youth of the ocean floor. Following the practice of an earlier theorist, J.H.F. Umbgrove, Hess called his speculations "geopoetry" as a concession to skeptics. Now that it no longer has such defensive duties to perform, and no one needs to be asked to suspend disbelief for the sake of the tale, we might be inclined to let it melt away along with the snows of yesteryear.

But should we? What better term for those moments of pure wonder when we contemplate even the most basic elements of planetary dwelling, and our words fumble in their attempts to do them justice? What else but 'geopoet' should we call Xenophanes, as he stands with the fossil of a seashell in his hand, in his mind the wild notion that the quarry he stands in once lay under the sea? What else should we call you as you watch the creek tug another bit of clay from the cutbank and feel a similar tug on your life? Or, for that matter, myself, trying to cobble together this strange sign system out of the varieties of our dumb astonishment?

The history of jazz, the history of Canada, local history, social history, clinical history, natural history, earth systems history, a brief history of time. The strain on the poor word, which displays itself dramatically by the time we get to Stephen Hawking's paradoxical title, has begun to show up, for me, at any rate, when we reach 'natural history'. I think it's because history really is intimately as well as etymologically connected with 'story', and 'story' always means human events – human events which unfold in a shapely manner. They have beginnings and ends we can count on; they create little homesteads for us that, whether inflected comically or tragically, colonize flux.

But when we turn to any event in the 'natural world' – a wave on a beach or a snowfall on a street – the safety of story is under constant threat. At any moment, we realize, this fragile structure can open out into the continuous metamorphoses of deep time, the implied camera chucking the responsibilities to its supposed subjects to skinny dip in the cosmos. A natural historian has to trot quickly through phrases like "in only a few million years" and "the mass extinctions of the Permian," lest the reader pause too long and begin to sink in her own wonderment. All historians, we might say, have to cope with rogue elements which threaten to invade the narrative. But the natural historian puts herself in harm's way; she can't remain safely within the stockade, but must venture out among the bears, the lichens and the aeons, risking geopoetry at every turn.

> There is a concept that corrupts and upsets all others.
> I refer not to Evil, whose limited realm is that of ethics;
> I refer to the infinite.
>
> JORGE LUIS BORGES

If^n: are all fears, at bottom, fears of endless uninflected time? That is, fears of being subject to a temporality we are unable to enfold in a human scheme? Is infinity not so much a vexatious mathematical concept as a name for the terrible frisson we feel when some familiar structure begins to quake?

In José Saramago's *All the Names*, the protagonist, Senhor José, is a Kafkaesque archivist who works at the Central Registry. Here all the data controlling social existence is housed and dispensed, an emblem of absolute bureaucracy. But beyond the orderly files which govern the living, the registry reaches back into long shelves of files for the dead, recesses where no one ventures, where the order disintegrates into heaps of documents, weighty and mysterious, like the anonymous strata in a formation of shale. Here is how Saramago describes the fear Senhor José feels as he breaks the rules and ventures among them:

. . . it was as if the spaces around him had suddenly grown larger, freer, stretching to infinity, as if the stones of the registry building were just the inert material from which they were made . . .

Senhor José is experiencing the vertigo which can afflict us when stone suddenly and unexpectedly reverts to rock, when we are not simply astonished, as in moments of geopoetic insight, but petrified.

Big fish have not always eaten little fish, since they have not always been equipped to do so. The appearance of jaws in the late Silurian must have shocked the oceans of the day even more severely than the release of *Jaws* shocked filmgoers and bathers in the mid-seventies. How did jaws come about? From the evidence of shark fossils, it appears that they evolved from the skeletal structure that supported the gills, so the passage of life forms into serious predation – the rhythm of chasing and escaping which determines so much of our existence as mammals – involved the shift from a breathing apparatus to a biting one.

This is mysterious enough, but not the end of it. Who, trapped in an endless meeting (departmental, political, familial) has not – heartlessly, traitorously – reversed evolution to imagine the jaw folded back into the gill, and dreamt of those speechless reaches of the Ordovician, the Cambrian, even the Proterozoic with its mute prokaryotes?

A *katabasis*, as the word comes down to us from the Greek, is a retreat following a defeat, from the interior of a country to its coast, like the retreat after the Greeks' defeat at Cunaxa. Katabatic winds follow roughly the same route, forming at the centre of an ice sheet where the air, cooled and made dense by constant contact with the ice, falls down the slope of the glacier toward its extremities, picking up speed as it goes. E.C. Pielou, in *After the Ice Age*, points out that katabatic winds must have been constant at the edge of the retreating glaciers, much as they are now at some Antarctic stations, where the mean windspeed is around 156 km per hour.

To experience such wind is to feel the full weight of winter, winter so profound it has broken from the other seasons and no longer even registers their absence; it is to understand winter as a regime rather than a phase. A katabatic wind speaks directly to the bones, passing through flesh quick as an x-ray. Sometime it speaks in one of the dialects of arthritis, and sometimes in that seductive numbness that persuades the lost trapper to lie down in the snow, to forsake the one-thing-after-another struggles of seasonal life and embrace his own eternal stillness.

I imagine quite a few people have heard waterfalls or rapids break into speech, and some of us have even heard ourselves addressed by name. I recall one occasion when, camped by a portage on the Goulais River, I woke to hear a throng of excited voices all shouting at once, and though I couldn't understand the language (Algonkian? Urdu?) it was clear that an important discovery had been made and that I should get up to join the general jubilation. Every so often, out of the hubbub, my name would appear, inflected by the accents of the mystery language, its vowel hollowed out and lichened with strange diacritical marks. This was not the first time the tent had worked like a magical ear, but knowing this did not prevent me from stumbling outside and making my way to the river's edge. By the time I could see their white curls in the darkness, the rapids had shifted back into their old protomusical purl and rush – very beautiful in itself, but not even remotely addressed to me, or anyone. Such experiences may have to do with dream mind bleeding into waking mind. Or it may be that, since we are doggedly linguistic as a species, our brains naturally process any continuous sound as a language. And since we are also, as a species, lonely, we are primed to hear ourselves called by name. Just the same, the illusion – if that's the word – was compelling, and the sense of loss, when the rapids reverted to ordinary water music, was acute.

So what does all this have to do with limestone? Why does this memory come to mind when, browsing along a limestone cliff or outcrop, I happen upon fossils embedded in the rock? I think it's the sudden emergence of a coiled symmetry, an apparent artfulness that calls across the eons, a compelling visual equivalent to being summoned out into the cold air of northern Ontario by one of its middle-sized rapids. Perhaps the appearance of the brachiopod or trilobite is even more dramatic because limestone usually seems so, well, *bland*, so *pierre ordinaire*. In Auden's poem in its praise, limestone is mutable stone that "responds"; it endorses the basic fabric of human life, and does not confront us with mythic extremities, as granite does, or lava, "whose blazing fury could not be fixed." So, when you come across a fossil, it seems a visual anomaly, a form as compelling as a signature in the grey matrix of the rock; it's as though you'd been spoken to, or called. And even though you know, as fact, that limestone is formed from the shells of many crustaceans compacted and fused over the millennia, the truth of this preposterous notion may only register when you trace, with your own sceptical finger, the elegant spiral of an ammonite whose shape has persisted among the pulverized, anonymous, remains of its fellows.

"Molten rock" – an oxymoron, surely, and perhaps no less impossible, no less a breach of common sense after we have watched a lava flow on film or visited Iceland to see for ourselves. We need something besides observation and explanation to help us cope with the vertigo produced by this conceptual dissonance, something that allows the paradox its truth, that is alive to its resonance with other aspects of our difficult dwelling amid flux. As a companion to the geology textbook I propose the fragments of Herakleitos, the sage who, it might be said, injected axiomatic language with the live air of the koan.

The ordering, the same for all, no god or man has made, but ever was and will be: everliving fire, kindled in measures and in measures going out.

During an ice age, sheets of ice that are miles deep fill in the valleys and cover most of the mountains. But some peaks – nunataks – poke through, while the glacier inches past, carving out amphitheatrical cirques and fanged arêtes, ploughing V-shaped valleys into U-shaped ones. Because of this experience the vision from a nunatak is different from those engendered by the summits of either romanticism or religion, on which the poet or prophet has generally transcended time to experience an epiphany, and generally in a single visionary flash. Nunatak visions are by contrast quantitative, requiring a commitment of twenty thousand years or so, and, rather than transcending or compacting time, tend to impress us with its corrosive power and conspicuous inattention to the designs of humans, or those of any other mere life form. One year more snow falls than melts, followed by another and another, ice filling the valley, encasing your Toyota and carrying it off with the other erratics. Two thousand years ago we drank the last of the coffee. Wasn't there some story about a girl who got carried off to the underworld and – what comes next? Anything?

When it comes to selecting an afterlife for oneself, almost no one chooses oblivion. But then no one is really one, either, and there's a real possibility that different parts, or aspects, of the self would choose different modes of final repose. The soul, we can safely assume, chooses eternity in one or another of its guises. The persona, probably, elects to live on in history through the agency of the name it went by, which survives on a gravestone, and maybe, if the persona has managed to store up fame or funds, in books.

But the spirit's choice isn't so obvious. Jack Gilbert observes that, though the soul is lodged, firmly, under the ribs, the spirit comes and goes. And, I would add, when we're lucky enough to be favoured with a visit, there are some unwritten rules we need to keep in mind. One is that neither it nor the moment should be named; another, that we should never ask, like some anxious parent, how long it plans to stay this time, nor lay heavy trips about its infrequent letters.

That's when it comes. When it goes, I'm guessing, it goes to the rivers no one knows; it goes to the mountains that have not been named. It chooses oblivion.

—and when, after I've wasted a lifetime looking,
picking over eskers, browsing beaches, rock shops, slag,
when, after I've up and quit, you suddenly
adopt me, winking from the gravel of the roadside
or the rip-rap of the trail
or the jewels of the rich;
when you shed your wilderness and move in,
living in my pocket as its sage, as my third,
uncanny testicle, the wise one,
the one who will teach me to desire
only whatever happens;
when you happen in my hand as nothing
supercooled to glass, as the grey
watersmooth rock that slew Goliath or the stone
no one could cast; when you come
inscribed by glaciers, lichened, mossed,
packed with former lives inside you
like a dense mass grave;

                   when you cleave,
when you fold,
when you gather sense as *omphalos, inukshuk,*
cromlech, when you rift in the stress
of intolerable time;

when you find me
as the moon found Li Po
in his drunken boat,
when you speak to my heart
of its heaviness, of the soft
facts of erosion, when you whisper in that
tongueless tongue it turns out,
though it can't be,
we both know—

Is there a word better fitted to its sense? The tough anglo-saxon syllable chirps into the air, wren-like and plosive, itself 'an indication of the presence of life.' We have all been touched to the quick at one time or another, and some of us have been quick with child: if all words worked this well we might do without metaphor.

But, to state the obverse of Yogi Berra's aphorism, when it's over, it's over. Either we're quick or, so it seems, we're dead – a word which stops down sound as surely as its opposite snaps it into being. It is against this duality, I think, that poetry has always struggled, seeking after pause, the place where the quick of existence and the blank duration of infinity are held in equipoise, perhaps – can we believe it? – even listening to each other. Adam Zagajewski says that poetry allows us "to experience astonishment and to stop in that astonishment for a long moment or two." Poetry is the pause where we turn toward stone, the breathless room where, by stratagems of language and mind, the quick and the infinite meet.

What is the difference between a rock and a stone? Had we been proceeding logically, this issue would have come first. Many will say there is no difference. But if we ask a geologist, the answer comes out pat: a stone is a rock that's been put to use: stone hammer, rip-rap, gravel, wall, paving stone, tombstone, milestone, statue. Now, a geopoet, I surmise, will give the same answer, but where the geologist snaps a lid shut, the geopoet opens Pandora's box. What happens between rock and stone is simply everything human, from the modifications necessary to make homes to, at the other extreme, the excesses of ownership and exploitation which submit all ends to ours. So another answer might be: rock is as old as the earth is; stone is only as old as humanity.

When I walk along the deactivated logging road that borders Loss Creek at the south end of Vancouver Island, I am also walking along a seam in the planet known as the Loss Creek – Leech River Fault. On the south side of the creek lies the bunched mafic muscle of the Crescent Terrane, a seamount formed from volcanoes erupting under the ocean, then carried by its underlying plate into a collision with North America. Most of B.C. is formed by such exotic terranes – twenty of them – crashing into the continental plate, and the Crescent Terrane is simply, at forty million years ago, the most recent. Before all these immigrants landed, the continent ended, and the Pacific began, at Calgary. Of course each collision altered the terranes which had collided earlier, like cars crashing into the wreckage of previous car crashes.

On the north side of the creek lies the Pacific Rim Terrane, which had arrived (the rather understated term is 'docked') only fifteen million years earlier, and so had little time to settle down before it was rear-ended by the Crescent Terrane. In outcrops and roadcuts you can see how the impact forced its beds into the air, and metamorphosed them into schists and argyllites. They actually do look alarmed, startled and vulnerable. Between the two terranes, there is rubble from each, large and small basaltic rocks mixed with the wafers of schist, all of them continuously licked by Loss Creek, which is persisting in the work begun yesterday in the ice age. But that's another story.

When you add time to rock, so I read, you shift from the rigid solid we know so well to the condition of viscous liquid. As I sit beside Loss Creek, a round piece of basalt in one hand, a flat disk of schist in the other, I'm sensing some such shift in myself. What I recall, specifically, is sitting by a campfire during a canoe trip in northern Quebec and being told (truthfully) that our twelve-year-old arses were resting on the oldest rock on the planet. That was, as I think back to the black lake reflecting the cold innumerable stars, with the same cold seeping up from the bald rock, to be overwhelmed and reassured at once. Though probably, the way things looked, we would one day die, the Precambrian granite which cupped the lake was unmoving, fixed, eternal.

But the absolute is not what it was.

When it comes to dream, it is difficult to tell the truth in prose. The narrative carries the dream reluctantly, like a butler required to serve tea to a gypsy, a gypsy who – oh dear – is claiming to be his mother. He looks offstage, mutely, at the writer. Is this really necessary? You can feel the narrative-butler losing faith in the project, embarrassed by the bad taste – the petticoats, the décolletage, the expressionistic lipstick – then embarrassed at his own dismal performance, his dereliction of duty in keeping up the pretence, and then a further, per-haps final embarrassment at the growing suspicion that she really is his mother and he's been behaving like a pompous ass.

Reading about even great dreams (and I'm thinking in particular of an amazing dream in the philosopher's stone genre) I feel sorry for the prose. It's not necessarily poetry that I'd bring to the res-cue, and it's certainly not stream-of-consciousness, that sad mime. What's needed is more like chat, especially one of those post-dream breakfast conver-sations, with lots of coffee and something out of the ordinary – pancakes, eggs Benedict, huevos ranche-ros. It's storytelling, not story, that serves dream best. And not public, mythic storytelling, either. Dream needs, and you know what, and then all of a sudden it wasn't a train but some sort of a raft with no side rails, and you, you bastard, were trying to shove me off into the ocean.

So: I wish I'd either dreamt the great philosopher's stone dream or been to breakfast with its dreamer, so I could talk it over hot from the unconscious. Here's how it goes in prose, as recorded in June Singer's *Boundaries of the Soul*:

> I am walking with a woman slightly older than myself along a mountain path. It is a glacial idyllic scene by moonlight. I am also somehow watching myself. We come to some huge gray boulders. They are blocking our path. We stop, and she turns to me and looks at me. We are engaged in pleasant conservation. Suddenly she turns extremely ugly. Her face takes on a greenish colour and she turns suddenly very old. I realize there is only one way to help the situation and that is to have intercourse with her. My penis enters her vagina then goes through her body and into the rock behind her. Then she disappears and I am alone, having intercourse with the rock.

Of course there is no difficulty for the Jungian interpreter in seeing the anima guiding the dreamer into the bedrock of an eventually integrated self.

But I'm thinking of lots of questions that would surface in that imagined breakfast chat (not to mention exclamations) and responses from my own bank of memories. How the granite of the shield, polished by waves and glaciers, often seems to be playing erotic variations on mammal form, with lots of emphasis on hip and breast, reaching toward us, while suggesting that there are plenty of other evolutionary paths that mammals might have taken. How it seems that the unconscious may be the one place we can meet rock without it turning, at our slightest touch or glance, into stone. When you make love to the rock, I'm guessing, it stays rock. It's you that changes.

Alternating layers of coarse and fine sediment that have
accumulated in an ancient lake and hardened into rock.
The coarse layers accumulated during the summer months
as streams carried silt and sand into the lake; the fine layers
formed each winter when the surface was covered with ice,
so that only slim grains of clay could settle to the bottom.

As I approach the high sandstone cliff with its
stacked, individual, terribly numerable varves, I
think of George from group, who was unable either
to stop collecting newspapers or to throw them out.
He would describe – not without some pride, or at
least amazement at his own extremity – how his
basement, then living room, then bedroom had
over the years become filled in with stacks of the
Globe and Mail, The Sun and the *Glengarry News*,
all layered sequentially until he was reduced to living in middle parts of his hallway and kitchen, his
life all but occluded by sedimented public time.
Unlike George's collection (which of course I saw
only in my mind's eye), the cliff's is open to eroding
elements, so that bits have fallen off to form a talus
slope of flat, wafer-like platelets at its base. This
one in my hand has been clearly imprinted by a
leaf – simple, lanceolate, probably an ancestor of

our ash or elder. Published but vestigial, gone like an anonymous oriental poet, its image still floating on the coarse grains of summer.

On the flip side, winter. Under the eyelid of the ice. How often I thought of writing you, but the pen hung over the page. All the details on the desk too shy to be inscribed. To settle, to hesitate exquisitely, at last to lie, zero among zeroes. Much listening then, but no audience. Rhetoric elsewhere. Language itself has long since backed out of the room on tiptoe.

Sometimes we believe that we must diagnose the perils of the winter varve, and so do our talk-show hosts and shrinks, who number its shades and phases as though it were pregnancy *renversé*, with suicide at the end instead of a baby. As though death were really death. As though the unspoken were failure. Having misread even the newspapers. Having been deaf to the music of the beech leaves, who will cling to their branches until spring, their copper fading to transparency, making a faint metallic clatter.

"To find a stronger word for love, a word that would be like wind, but from under the earth, a word that doesn't need mountains, but enormous caves in which it houses. . . ." So Elias Canetti articulates our deep longing for oracle, the wind from the earth, the wind within the rock. We long for such a word as lovers, but also as language users; the desire takes us to that moment when words – which have always been so full of their own energies, so juiced on the buzz of abstraction – turn, with a sense of their insufficiency, toward rock.

Walk comes to the aid of words here. The rhythms of walking, whether it's a hike, a pilgrimage, or a stroll, let language be in the body, give it access to physical being. They mediate between the anxious, inadequate words in our heads and the silent, oracular, earth. As Margaret Avison puts it –

> To walk the earth
> is to be immersed,
> slung by the feet
> in the universe.

Will this produce a "stronger word for love"?

Maybe not. But it helps us to realize, on behalf of our faithful words, that their greatest eloquence lies in their failure.

Xenophanes of Colophon (sixth century BCE) is known for his attack on the anthropomorphic gods of Homer (if cattle, horses, and lions had hands, they would draw gods like cattle, horses, and lions) and his contention that, on the contrary, there is "one god, greatest among gods and men, in no way similar to mortals either in body or in thought." That is to say, I think, that whatever god or gods may be, they are inaccessible to myth, or, indeed, language. And perhaps more telling still is his view that human knowledge is restricted to what *seems* to be, and that "No man knows, or will ever know, the truth about the gods."

Besides this chastening of anthropomorphism and curbing of the extent of human knowledge, Xenophanes is credited with being the first palae-ontologist. Observing fossils of seaweed and fish in a quarry near Syracuse, and either observing or hearing about others at Malta and Pharos, he inferred that the earth had been configured differently in times past, and that it must undergo cycles of wet and dry periods. It was during a passage of relative wetness, when the world was covered with mud, that the ancient shells and impressions had been left. Usually this fragment is taken to show the early use of evidence to support theory, another small step on the way to Aristotle and the birth of science.

But suppose we think of Xenophanes as a geo-poet rather than as either a proto-scientist or a naive cosmologist. It is certainly true that poetry was his medium, and that he used the Homeric hexameter to, among other things, dispute the Homeric world view. Suppose we also credit Xenophanes with the poet's capacity for wonder and decreation; suppose that, in the quarry with the fish fossil at his fingertips, he is not only astute but astonished. Isn't it likely that, having sensed the power of undomesticated time, he would naturally go on to remove the projection of our image onto gods? And, having seen its assumptions shattered by a fish swimming in limestone, insist on the strict limits of our knowing?

All over the world, caves – including the famous ones at Lascaux – have been connected in the mythic imagination with wombs, and yonic symbols (cleft, downward-pointing triangles) carved at their entrances by Stone Age people. These must be among the most eloquent of human signs: they name the earth as mother, and declare an intimate analogue between her body and ours. To carve one of these was a powerful, yearning, anthropocentric act.

Standing at the other end, perhaps, of artistic complexity is James Joyce's use of the symbol in the "Oxen of the Sun" sequence in *Ulysses*, where its mundane representation (if you can hypothesize such a thing in the midst of the baroque clutter of the piece) is the triangle on a bottle of Bass beer. This humble, very Irish, symbol might be said to ground the vertiginous accumulation of references to procreation, gestation, and birth, structured on the nine months of pregnancy, which are rendered as successive styles of English prose from early translations to current American slang – current in 1904, that is. No one, including A.M. Klein, the great poet who first "broke the code" of the sequence, could fail to be impressed by Joyce's virtuoso variations on the symbol. But is his achievement, at bottom, any more brave, or daring, or hopeful than that of our Stone Age ancestor carving the feminine glyph into the rock?

Nothing is absence under the auspices of eternity; zero, on the other hand, is absence which slides into mind because it has intimations of infinity – intimations that are undomesticated by arithmetic. The nothing that comes of nothing, as Lear learns to his pain, is tragedy – that is, ruin cut exactly to the dimension of the human.

But zero is a moon without metaphors.

3

Waiting for Shay

For the first half of the twentieth century, logging rail-roads were the most common means of hauling timber out of the forest to booming grounds on the coast. By 1924 there were 74 logging railroads operating on Vancouver Island, and at least two thirds of them used the powerful, dependable Shay locomotive.

(i)

Summon it from sea mist: a dark shape
afloat on its barge in the half-air half-
water dreamtime of the coast. It may seem
a sort of monument, possibly a squashed Rodin
or the Vienna Philharmonic smelted down,
containerized and shipped on a drawn-out
tremulous Wagnerian chord, *frisson*,
foreboding, liebestod, up the strait
toward us. What is coming, we might ask, as the mist
lifts a flirtatious hem to give a glimpse
of massive body, petrified
rhinoceros or else some manic futurist's
reclining nude. On the shore
among the bristling Sitka spruce the mist is fingerless
caress, taking leave and entering, continuously
making threshold out of edge. And the forest, does it sense
the coming of another brand of predator
out there on the strait? Is this just
another beetle in a string of permutations
variously carapaced and horned, something
that might burrow, make place
for itself and propagate and lend its pattern
to the weave the way engraver beetles
leave a writing in the wood?

Does the forest simply go on making moss
and rot and whispering translations of translations, rain
into leaf into berry into bear as Shay
slides by on the tide?

(ii)

Engine, ingenuity: how could we not love it?
Four-fifths animal, eats wood and water, breathes,
whistles, relieves itself of pressure with a sigh,
and harnesses the power of the sneeze to haul
its mass of gears and rods and
big avuncular belly up the ridge. Asthmatic,
cheerful, clockwork-clever,
tough as a troll, tough as a suit of armour that has long
outlived its knight, Shay is for sure
the brand-new neolithic monster for the job.

(iii)

At the booming ground the wharf
extends its arm. The tracks reach
up the river valley as its spurs will also
reach up tributary creeks to make a stiff
tree-diagram that imitates the watershed
in iron. Waiting for Shay.
When the barge arrives the sleeping shape
will wake and start to breathe and
build a head of steam, accumulating wrath
like a hell-fire preacher. Then,
in a series of sharp
expostulations – work work work –
crank itself ashore. And then
the clock's wound up.

4

Five Ways to Lose Your Way

(i)

How can you be lost, I ask myself, how, on a fine showery-with-sun Saturday afternoon, how can you, the seeker, more than that, the questor, the ardent archaeologist of missing logging locomotives, a man equipped with topographic maps and lunch and a copy of Tomas Tranströmer's *Collected Poems* as well as a clear mental image of the Vulcan 0-4-0 saddle tank locomotive that rumour has it is up here on the ridge turning into a humped hill or tumulus, sleeping its charmed sleep among the second growth hemlock and deadfall, all that bulk healed over with step-moss, with alder thicket, with lichens of every race and colour, its cast-iron work ethic rusting in the persistent mist fumbling up the ridge from the strait, one end of the boiler maybe gone to make a cave for bears, you can see them, Mama Bear, Papa Bear, Little Baby Bear, snoozing the winter away inside the carcass of the myth of progress, and truly this is the kind of romantic dumbass thinking that got you up here in the first place and off the path as though to say who needs it, it's just over there behind that outcrop or maybe if you cut across this salal-filled gully, sure and *what* direction did you say the highway was, o Parsifal of locomotives lost, how can you be lost, how can I even ask, you were a little clot of lostness looking for a place to happen, stepping up the old overgrown road like a man stepping blindly into line one of *The Inferno*, a man clueless enough to obey the siren call of a putative logging locomotive conjured by railroad nuts whose desire for a relic is so intense it summons large mechanical chimeras out of shabby second-growth and lures hapless fools from the path to thrash gracelessly through purgatories of deadfall. That's how, that's who, and when it comes to you, sucker, lost is too good a word.

Although it presents itself as a question, How Can
You Be Lost has, as we have seen, no lasting alle-
giance to the interrogative form. It's as though the
words had rushed into the prefrontal lobe when
the realization struck, as it were, from the rear, and
grabbed whatever mood was handy on the way past,
much as a naked person startled from bed does not
pause to quibble over the choice of dressing gown,
sweatpants, jeans, or shorts. At the first sick surge of
lostness the interrogative gets to work dividing self
from self, finding a *you* to interrogate among the
glum bureaucracies of *I*, then isolating this incom-
petent idiot in the desiccating winds of incredulity.
How Can You Be Lost? Now the mood is free to
harden into its rhetorical form, well known from
childhood, when the air is thick with questions
intended to compel behaviour rather than elicit
a response. Indeed, as the child discovers, any attempt to reply fuels the wrath of the parent, who
has been waiting for just such an injection of rhyth-
mic energy (*what* did you say?) and now has access
to an even finer fury. From the upper reaches of
the rhetorical question it is but a short step into true
exclamation, the mood in which each word, by an

elegant reversal of the original interrogative lift, falls with the blunt redundancy of a piledriver timed to correspond to whatever vain efforts – thrashing, say, or slogging – the organism may be making in the problematical outer world, the semantic content of the phrase beaten thinner and thinner with each iteration, until it at last achieves the condition of pure spondaic punctuation: ! ! ! ! !

How can you be lost in a bush so thoroughly flagged with orange neon tape you'd think it was a crime scene or the route of some future right-wing protestant parade. Its tutelary ghosts have long since fled, abandoning the bush to politics and publicity. You approach one hemlock, who looks ashamed to be so singled out, so shorn of anonymity, and inspect its orange necktie. "Falling Boundary" it reads, and now you see how all the orange-taped trees form a rough line, standing among their fellows as though, having been sentenced, they are nevertheless still hanging around in hell's waiting room, leafing through out-of-date issues of *Time*. Now you notice another line of trees flagged with yellow tape marked "Road Location," and since this seems to imply destination, you start off in that direction. "Follow the yellow tape road," you hum as you duck and clamber, hitching over fallen trunks and beating your way through blackberry canes. But is this such a good idea? Think of those logging roads left inscribed on hillsides like x-rays of the intestines, all that forking and switchbacking, they're as bad as artful upper-class suburbs. Who knows what Byzantine design the wizard of falling has in mind?

Who gets seduced by this kind of signal anyhow, it's like expecting a sign announcing "To the Treasure" when you arrive on the island. Sure enough, if it isn't Dorothy and the Tin Woodman shambling toward you down the proto-road, looking about 14 and 300 respectively, and some pissed off, tripping over each other and pretty snippy with their 'Do watch where you're going Tinny dear' and 'My aren't we the touchy homecoming queen' palaver. He's been chopping since 1906 looking for a heart inside each stump, no, no, no, no; now he thinks he might settle for a nice pair of tin testicles, he's not getting any younger, not to mention the dwindling resource, not to mention the goddam Americans with their unfair subsidy this and their dumping that, not to mention the rust which is seizing his joints and widening the holes in his torso, all in all he's feeling the way you'd expect some Vulcan saddle tank locomotive that's been left out in the rain for seventy odd years to feel. Meanwhile, as she draws closer, it becomes clear that Dorothy has been only partly successful in sustaining the illusion of youth, and now looks like a child movie star and the child's ruthless mother at the same time, her Golly Toto charm hardened into a policy of Kansas at any cost. You might as well sit on a stump and watch them flounder past. You wonder whether Toto has been eaten by a cougar; you wonder how many of these pseudo-paths his mistress will have to follow, and whether falling, contrary to the assurance of the orange tape, isn't infinite. Knowing that if you simply stay where you are a familiar plot is going to take shape around you, populated by inadequate animals and talking tools, with a director so obviously fake only a fool like you, and only for a running time of approximately one hour and fifty-eight minutes, could manage to suspend his soggy, dog-eared disbelief.

How can you be lost? When the incredulity fades, when the anger damps down, when the fear diminishes from clamour to drone, the question may be open to receive other inflections, other echoes. The question may finally *be* a question. You think of Hamlet telling Horatio that there are more things in heaven and earth than are dreamt of in his philosophy, how entire readings of the play can depend on which word receives the emphasis. Sitting on your stump in the middle of a clearcut-to-come, you reflect on the paradox embedded in the common expression 'to get lost': you can't get lost any more than you can fall asleep. Lostness gets you; sleep gathers you inward to itself. But being lost – can a person dwell in such a space, somewhere outside the ubiquity of plans, the falling boundaries and logging roads projected into the future? Deep in your backpack, Tomas Tranströmer murmurs of that nearly-discovered country between wakefulness and sleep, of Schubert's music catching an entire life in a few ordinary chords, of a clearing which can only be found by someone who is lost.

The rain, after you've watched it for a while,
seems to discover stillness in itself and,
though it keeps on falling,
pauses. Each drop
equivocates and would,
were it possible, ebb back
up its plummet. The rain looks rumpled,
slept-in, an old coat hung mid-air
remembering the body which once
gave it shape. We are but a hair's breadth
from the birth of cedar, who will soon be stepping
through its curtain dressed as a tall
shaggy animal, with arms that reach and droop and
catch the drips in splayed green hands like stylized
amphibians. Each gesture steps toward us.
Already it is roof. Already you can rest
your weight against its trunk and think of
living in the company of soft
hospitable fibres, houses, chests,
canoes. You can imagine humming your old
five-note phrase with a lilt that
lifts it toward wren song – how can you
be lost – and lets it go into the rain's
inexhaustible slang.

5

Approaching the Clearing

When we come to contemplate a place for creativity in the outer world, most of us imagine a room in a house (a garret, an attic, a nook), or maybe a room that is a house (a studio, a shed, a cabin). These interiors not only ensure seclusion and protect the artist from routine busy-ness, they are also places where intimations from far off may be received, where hunches can hop from their burrows to browse, and favourite objects and souvenirs can unfold, without embarrassment, toward the privileged condition of icons. Whether spare and zen-like or cluttered with drafts and the remains of yesterday's lunch; whether fully wired or scrupulously off-line; whether a virtual greenhouse of windows or enclosed as a chrysalis, these are places where tentative intuitions can move safely toward material expression. Within the walls of the otherwise sensible house, one room is reserved for the unexpected, the untamed thought. It is the opposite of an office.

I think that the clearing is the wild ancestor of this room of one's own. It precedes that room in the same way astonishment precedes, and provokes, poetry. Before we experience the need for a room devoted to the imagination, we experience the need for room itself, a place where the sky meets the earth. That is how we experience a clearing when walking through the forest, as a pool of light where the trees relent, a place that combines seclusion with openness. As we approach, we tend to slow down and shut up, partly because of a possible deer or fox, and partly out of a respect for the presence which always seems to gather in a clearing. Each has its own character, its own tone. I suspect that sense of presence is the true ancestor of our notion of place, before arbitrary naming and the grid.

So we enter tentatively, craning our senses, much as a deer or fox would. It is as though we had entered our own listening. When we pause here, taking off our packs, getting out the water bottles and binoculars, it is in a spirit of cohabitation rather than ownership. We can give attention to other creatures – kinglets in the fringe, ravens overhead, the spotted saxifrage growing in the rock, or to the granite itself – letting our minds, like zoom lenses, shift between the minute and the immense. Back in the room of my own, my imagination may hold sway like a child emperor or (on good days) like a generous host, but it does not have the immediate opportunity to experience itself as a creature among creatures, a being among beings. Such moments may be remembered and written in the room of one's own, but it is in the clearing that creativity first experiences that mental openness, vulnerability and wordlessness we call astonishment. The clearing is no one's room.

These moments, obviously, do not go on forever, and one of the things that brings them to a close (besides exigencies like getting back before dark) is an impulse I have come to call "cabinning." "Just suppose," I say to myself, or to a trail companion if I have one, "you were to build a cabin here. Where would you put it?" This impulse, which I'm assuming is not exclusive to me, may seem innocent enough, but it projects us into the clearing in a way that alters all the relationships inside it. All its aspects and creatures are now made to refer to this central perspective; the clearing becomes a site. "I placed a jar in Tennessee," says Wallace Stevens,

> And round it was, upon a hill
> It made the slovenly wilderness
> Surround that hill.

It is very difficult, if not impossible, for us to leave things alone, to avoid placing the jar or imagining the cabin. And although our motives may reveal themselves to us as a desire to protect and prolong the moment, to 'bring it home' and cherish it, such a gesture is the first step toward ownership. (Sitting Bull, referring to white settlers: "Their love of possessions is a disease among them.") When a real house or cabin is built in the clearing, the very fact of the building reduces wilderness, as Stevens' "slovenly" implies and colonial experience confirms. But within that house, there may still be a space which hearkens back to the clearing, a room devoted to recovering that open, unowned presence.

Among the rivers-and-mountains poets of ancient China, a common theme is that of travelling to visit a hermit and not finding him. In effect the poem becomes a small vessel for the details of the journey, and a means of gesturing toward the sage's 'telling without telling'. In a well-known example by Li Po, the poet attempts to visit a Taoist master in the Tai T'ien mountains. The translation is by Arthur Cooper.

> Where the dogs bark
> by roaring waters,
> Whose spray darkens
> the petals' colours,
> Deep in the woods
> deer at times are seen;

The valley noon:
one can hear no bell,
But wild bamboos
cut across bright clouds,
Flying cascades
hang from jasper peaks;

No one knows
which way you have gone:
Two, now three pines
I have leant against!

We might think of this as an antidote to cabinning, or the equivalent of removing a jar from Tennessee.

Now suppose we try to approach the clearing from a different direction, imagining ourselves deep in the surrounding forest, labouring through deadfall, moving toward the opening up ahead where the gloom diminishes. On this approach I am carrying a copy of the fragments of Herakleitos in my backpack, and suggest we contemplate, as we clamber over fallen trunks and angle-step among the roots, one of them in particular. "Nature loves to hide" is the usual translation of *phusis kruptesthai philei*, an aphorism that can carry great power for us. Herakleitos is not saying that there are elements in nature, such as deer or the hermit thrush we glimpsed a moment ago, that conceal themselves; he makes the claim for nature in general. Speaking across such distances of culture and time, it may well throw into relief one of the root assumptions of Western culture, with its penchant for classification and control. The scientific response to Herakleitos – so immediate that, usually, no alternative can raise its voice – is to aggressively expose what is hidden, to place nature on the rack, as Bacon recommended, and force it to divulge its secrets. Of course, once they have been discovered, we put them to use for the betterment of humanity. And we can do this because nature is simply unfeeling matter, and can't 'love' anything.

But in Herakleitos, nature's love of concealment resounds in quite a different way. *Phusis*, routinely translated as 'nature', is a word which gestures to the deep character of a thing, in a sense compatible with the expressions 'human nature' and 'the nature of things'. Charles Kahn offers as an alternative translation "the true character of a thing likes to be in hiding". *Phusis* leans into ontology; it has to do with how things inhabit flux. And understanding nature this way inhibits the automatic responses of investigation, exposure and mastery. Hiddenness is by no means a privative condition; it by no means presents itself as a problem to be solved. That clearing we're headed for is not a 'solution' to the innumerable, hospitable concealments of the forest. In another fragment, Herakleitos says (as translated by Kahn) "The hidden attunement is better than the obvious one" (*harmoniē aphanēs phanerēs kreitton*), a beautifully gnomic, and in Greek intensely musical, aphorism. Besides reinforcing the positive value of concealment, it suggests that deep form is to be preferred over superficial structures, wherever they are found.

Approaching the clearing in the company of Herakleitos, we are bound to be reminded of his insight into the potent dynamic in which opposites engage, how intimately they are connected in the live web of *phusis*, "living each other's death, dying each other's life." It was partly out of reflections on Herakleitos that Martin Heidegger developed his understanding of truth as "unconcealment" (*aletheia*), a condition which, as the word implies, requires a preceding hiddenness, requires in fact a matrix of being that does not make itself manifest, and out of which it opens. The work of art, for Heidegger, occurs in that tension. As George Steiner, an extremely lucid guide to the turnings and returnings of Heidegger's thought, sums it up: "It is the work of art that shows us that 'truth happens' in the primordial struggle between 'clearance' and 'concealment'."

We are still some distance from the clearing we set out for, and which, approached from this direction, we have come to see as an opening that is itself secluded, and that requires such seclusion to truly exist. I suggest that, instead of forging on ahead, we pause here by a moss-and-lichen covered cedar stump, drink some tea from the thermos, and reflect on the many forms of hiddenness we find among us, and – although this may be the work of a lifetime – within us as well.

"Deep in the forest there is an unexpected clearing which can only be reached by someone who has lost his way." This is the opening line of a prose poem by Tomas Tranströmer, and it offers another approach to the clearing – if approach is the word, since it removes from us the power to find it through our own volition. This is the clearing that cannot be sought, cannot be approached by the enquiring mind. It turns us back to ourselves, to a *via negativa* which embraces lostness and brings the hiddenness of the forest into ourselves. Indeed, as Tranströmer presents his clearing, we experience not sudden illumination but an increasing uncertainty: a group of large stones suggests the foundations of a house, but we can't be sure, and no one – now that the oral tradition has declined – remembers. Writing itself, seen from this perspective, is a means of forgetting. Tranströmer's own writing here, though superficially a narrative, proceeds in a series of poetic observations with overtones of folktale, parable and dream, outside the normal "communications network" to which the narrator, having found a path, finally returns.

Being lost: as though, in the course of the many exchanges between concealment and clearance, it is necessary that at one point concealment should be complete, free from our paths and thoughts, enfolding even the seeker into *phusis*. Let us imagine ourselves on a hike, having taken the wrong fork in the trail, having attempted to rectify our mistake by taking a shortcut that got us disoriented (I forgot the compass, you the GPS), having climbed a ridge for an overview which informed us that the sun was setting in the east, then found ourselves unable to find even path B. Now, when we arrive at the clearing, we will enter it shaken, hopeful, and brimming with vulnerability. The clearing will be completely itself, a wilderness outside the co-ordinates imposed by maps and plans. We will understand that the clearing is, before all else, a gift.

The approach to the clearcut is by logging road, and at times specified by the timber company to whom the forest is licensed. This one, Jordan River North Main, climbs from the Strait of Juan de Fuca up the ridge, taking it in a series of wrestling holds – a reach and twist diagonally across the slope, then another reach into a further more intimate grip. Tunnelling up, the forest pulling back on either side into its shadows, affecting to ignore our dust cloud, as it also affects to ignore the nailed-up numbers and plastic tape identifying cutblocks. Second gear, third, back to second, the car's voice urgent, clenched. Now and then a stream crashes down the hillside, gets directed through a culvert and released like a branded calf. While the road rushes on to take the next stretch of ridge.

We arrive into an openness that is too open, de-fenceless, stripped of shadow, a clearing that is no longer in relation to concealment, as though the live muscle of that opposition has been severed. All the details are debris: mud, stumps, branches pressed into caterpillar tracks or heaped in piles. We get out into nude sunlight. The car ticks as it cools. Someone has thrown an old kitchen cabinet onto the brush heap, as though to declare solidarity with the rubbles of family and war. It seems a place whose history happened all at once instead of bit by bit. It seems a place where history is all there is.

But I think it is important to pause here, too, if only to recall some of how that history unscrolled. I am thinking of the old-time loggers, of those photographs from the early days – the high rig-gers strapped to the trunks they were topping, the impossibility of that embrace, the brawn of it. Loggers posed on trophy logs, hands on hips, hat-ted, moustached, pipes clenched, looking like the cast of a musical called *Tall Timber*. The caption would identify them by vocation – fallers and buck-ers, chokermen, hooktenders, high rigger, donkey puncher, whistle punk – all the plosives and stops with which machines are loved in language. Before the days of the chainsaw, it was a popular thing to photograph two fallers standing on springboards on either side of a huge cedar or fir, holding their axes at slope arms, or in front with a gesture I recognize from portraits of rock stars presenting their guitars. I recall one in particular in which a wide wedge has been cut into the trunk, with a third logger lying in it, serene as St. Peter in a Russian icon. I wonder: is he being sheltered by its reach into the sky or swallowed by its downward plunge? They're still there, in my mind's eye, emblems like the magi imagined by Yeats, hovering outside the turbulence of history and work.

The donkey engine, the logging locomotive, the chainsaw and the logging truck: the industrialization of the forest progressed in a series of surges produced by the introduction of rugged ingenious machines. Let me focus on the chainsaw, since that is where I, like most Canadians, have a small dose of experience. The idea for an 'endless chain' goes back, in Canada at least, to 1918, when a man named James Shand of Dauphin, Manitoba observed how barbed wire would cut into a fence post when his horses leaned against the fence, and came up with the idea of marrying the crosscut saw and the bicycle. But it wasn't until the thirties, in Germany, that Andreas Stihl got the weight-to-horsepower ratio right and the chainsaw became sufficiently portable to use effectively in the bush. Stihl saws and the various knock-offs established themselves as the best around and had, by virtue of a fifteen-fold rise in production, all but replaced the crosscut saw by 1939. 'Hitlers', they were called.

Now, leaning against the car, I recall that mix of fear and exhilaration that are always present when I pick up the chainsaw. Whenever I lose my temper, this is where it goes to incubate. Yank the cord, it wakes, ready-to-hand, remorseless, effective as a hit man. That wise fear I feel before I get it cranked and revved turns into some sort of passive gear just waiting for its manic buddy to show up so they can roar off, mesmerized and gleeful. Those two are a bad combination. I especially remember the time when, thinning out a plantation of white spruce, I just kept on cutting past the end of a row, caught up in that snarl of power, and wound up taking down a bunch of red pines that grew alongside. Five of them fell before we ran out of gas. I stood there, in a clearing that was completely mine, holding the suddenly dead off-centre weight of a Homelite XL 130. I was, at that moment, a true citizen of the century.

Everything listening at me:
the stumps oozing resin, the birdsong
bouncing off my head like sonar,
the hammered air with its fading
after-echoes. I think of people
herded to a square, staring
at the man on the platform.
Whatever I say now
will be strictly interpreted
and parsed. Is this the way it works,
locking you, stunned, in the imperative,
making a weapon of each tool?
Why can't we just bury innocence instead of
wrecking it over and over, as if
it could never die
enough?
What I want to say is
somewhere a man steps
softly into a hemlock-and-fir fringed
pause. Heart full.
Head empty. His lost path
scrawls away behind him. A blue
dragonfly with double wings zags, hovers,
zags. A flicker he can't see
yucks its ghost laugh
into the thin slant light.

6

Deactivated West 100

On his first attempt he missed the turn – partly because he was unpractised in the art of reading bush roads, partly because he was worried about the oil pan, and partly because of the fog, which floated among the conifers. On the highway it had been the usual soup most of the way up the coast, thinning as he turned off onto the main logging road and began to climb, swimming up through the spruce and hemlock. Eventually he could see a faint pool of light ahead, an aura lifted from an Emily Carr and hung above the road, complete with the suggestion of rainbow hovering around the yolk-like centre. We're headed for a fog-dog, he thought, veering to avoid a pothole and re-addressing his attention to the road.

Surfacing through it was as abrupt as waking from a dream, the sky smack-blue and cloudless, a winter wren singing somewhere among the stumps, and no one else alive on earth. The fog lay below him, opulent and plump as blown-in insulation, filling the whole strait between the clearcut where he stood and the Olympic Mountains, which stuck up, it seemed, about a hundred yards away to the south. With a spotting scope you'd probably be able to make out the demigods lounging in the alpine meadows like indolent adolescents, breeding mischief out of too much boredom and power. No doubt the fog had been their idea. Behind him the car steamed in the sudden sunlight. They had missed the turn.

But today it was easy and obvious. A few yards after the turn, a sign declared the road deactivated – bridges torn out, culverts removed, delivered over to neglect. And a short way beyond, the crest where Loss Creek's valley falls suddenly away with that lurch made familiar by Westerns, always accompanied by the theme, now swollen from the inside by French horns, who have appeared from nowhere. *The Valley*. He sits a moment behind the wheel, recalling the aerial photograph with the two parallel ridges scored into the comfortable roundness of the hills like some hard-edged prehistoric canal. This is the line of geologic scrimmage, where one terrane, a young volcanic island something like Iceland, rammed into and under its predecessor. In the roadcut he can see the beds of schist which were tilted upright and metamorphosed in that slow crash. He leaves one self, stalled among hugenesses, in the car, while he takes the binoculars and begins to walk down the road into the valley.

It soon becomes clear that the valley is full of bears; either that or the few who live here always come up the road to shit, leaving dozens of plump berry-rich mounds like three-dimensional full stops. Many are impressively fresh. At each he pauses to scan the road and creek ahead, feeling that familiar mix of hope and fear, and noticing again that the breeze, blowing toward him, will not spread news of his arrival further down. Juncos jitter in the alders. A varied thrush sends its whistle-buzz to shake and dissolve in the nearly echoic air. He walks on.

She comes as a surprise. He's been looking toward a dark stump on which, he thinks, some thrush-like bird has landed. As he fiddles with the focus the stump acquires first a deep gloss, then hair, then the ability to move, which, to his alarm, she does. Only then, following the line of her gaze, does he notice the two cubs sitting in the middle of the road, sniffing and pawing at each other, still blessed with that spidery, nearly silly quality they enjoy before the full gravitas of being bear descends. The mother goes back to munching whatever is so succulent at the roadside, so rich in her gloss she seems lit from the inside. He watches them a long time through the binoculars, staring through a keyhole into the other world, where our deaths walk calmly among us, amiable hugs that browse its deactivated boulevards and cul-de-sacs.

Walking back toward the car he finds the bridge where Loss Creek enters the valley, so small, apparently, it was not worth tearing up. With a backward glance in the direction of the bears, he climbs down the embankment. So, he thinks, tell me about it. Thick thimbleberry bushes, foamflower speckling the ground, columbine blossoms floating like earrings with no ears. Here the creek is sleek and narrow, barely a brook. The upright beds of schist pass it, in a series of runnels and pools, from hand to hand, or perhaps leaf to leaf, since it more closely resembles the fanned-out pages of a book. The rock seems to have opened outward, as if the experience of tectonic catastrophe had left it with an awareness of its kinship – however slight – with the columbine and saxifrage in its crevices, and even with the creek which flows between its leaves, eliciting undertones of sage green from its darkness. Their talk is asyntactical, a small presocratic hubbub. A junco flies past him and under the bridge, tossing comments like pebble-dash; the occasional song of a Swainson's thrush postulates another stream that flows uphill; far off, and next door to the heart, the subliminal drumming of a grouse. And containing them all, the live silence of the valley, with its edges of acoustic rock and its core of impacted shadow – that place where lava cooled so fast it kept its muscle tone and passed directly into mammal, quickening, sitting up to sniff the breeze, and ambling off among the alders.

Auden, W.H. "In Praise of Limestone," *Collected Shorter Poems*. London: Faber and Faber, 1966.

Avison, Margaret. "Civility a Bogey," *Winter Sun*. Toronto: University of Toronto Press, 1960.

Berger, John. *And our faces, my heart, brief as photos*. New York: Pantheon, 1984.

Borges, Jorge Luis. *Labyrinths*. New York: New Directions, 1962.

Gilbert, Jack. *The Great Fires*. New York: Knopf, 1995.

Harrison, Robert Pogue. *Forests*. Chicago: University of Chicago Press, 1992.

Humphreys, Helen. "Installation," *Anthem*. London, Ontario: Brick, 1999.

Kahn, Charles. *The Art and Thought of Heraclitus*. Cambridge: Cambridge University Press, 1979.

Kramer, Samuel Noah. *History Begins at Sumer*. Philadelphia: University of Philadelphia Press, 1981.

Lane, Patrick. "Winter 45," *Winter*. Regina: Coteau, 1990.

Li Po. "On Visiting a Taoist Master in the Tai-T'ien Mountains and Not Finding Him," *Li Po and Tu Fu*. Trans. Arthur Cooper. New York: Penguin, 1973.

Pielou, E.C. *After the Ice Age*. Chicago: University of Chicago Press, 1991.

Saramago, José. *All the Names*. New York: Harcourt, 2000.

Singer, June. *Boundaries of the Soul*. New York: Anchor, 1994.

Steiner, George. *Heidegger*. London: Harvester Press, 1978.

Stevens, Wallace. "Anecdote of the Jar," *Collected Poems*. New York: Knopf, 1969.

Tranströmer, Tomas. "The Clearing," *New and Collected Poems*. Trans. Robin Fulton. Newcastle upon Tyne: Bloodaxe, 1997.

Weil, Simone. *Gravity and Grace*. Trans. Emma Craufurd. London: Routledge, 1963.

Zagajewski, Adam. *Another Beauty*. Trans. Clare Cavanagh. New York: Farrar Strauss, 1998.

◆ ACKNOWLEDGEMENTS

"Otherwise Than Place" first appeared in *The Eye in the Thicket*, edited by Sean Virgo (Saskatoon: Thistledown, 2002) ❡ "Between Rock and Stone" appeared in *The Antigonish Review* ❡ "Five Ways to Lose Your Way" was first published as a chapbook by Jack Pine Press. Thanks to all these publishers. The excerpt from "Civility a Bogey" from Margaret Avison's *Always Now, The Collected Poems* [three volumes] (Erin, Ontario: The Porcupine's Quill, 2003) has been reprinted courtesy of the author ❡ The excerpt from "Winter 45" from Patrick Lane's *Winter* (Winnipeg: Coteau, 1990) has been reprinted, courtesy of the author ❡ The excerpt from Robert Pogue Harrison's *Forests* (Chicago: University of Chicago Press, 1992) has been reprinted with the permission of the publisher ❡ "On Visiting a Taoist Master in the Tai-T'ien Mountains and Not Finding Him" from *Li Po and Tu Fu*, translated by Arthur Cooper (London: Penguin Classics, 1973) is copyright © Arthur Cooper, 1973 and has been reprinted by permission of the publisher.

Thanks to Stan, Tim, Sean, Jane and Dotter for their careful attention to individual pieces, to Jan for ongoing listening and discussion, and to Clare, who edited the whole manuscript with a fine and scrupulous ear.

◆ A NOTE ON THE TYPE

Electra was designed for machine composition by the American type designer W.A. Dwiggins (1880–1956) and released by the Mergenthaler Linotype Company in 1935. Although Electra was originally issued with a sloped roman italic, Dwiggins added a cursive italic in 1940 which is preferred by many typographers. This book was set using Adobe's digital revival of Electra and its cursive italic.

Typeset in Electra by Andrew Steeves
& printed offset at Gaspereau Press.

Gaspereau Press acknowledges the support of the Canada Council
for the Arts, the Nova Scotia Department of Tourism & Culture,
and the Government of Canada through the Book Publishing
Industry Development Program.

1   3   5   7   9   8   6   4   2

Library & Archives Canada Cataloguing in Publication

McKay, Don, 1942–
Deactivated west 100 / Don McKay.
Essays and poems.

ISBN 1-55447-009-9 (bound)
ISBN 1-55447-008-0 (pbk.)

1. Poetry.   2. Nature in literature.   I. Title.
PS8575.K28D42 2005   C811'.54   C2005-903496-3

GASPEREAU PRESS PRINTERS & PUBLISHERS
47 CHURCH AVENUE, KENTVILLE, NOVA SCOTIA
CANADA B4N 2M7   WWW.GASPEREAU.COM